6/99
CL

AGH9998-1

Why Does My Tummy Rumble When I'm Hungry?
and other questions about the digestive system

by

Sharon Cromwell

Photographs by

Richard Smolinski, Jr.

Series Consultant

Dan Hogan

RIGBY INTERACTIVE LIBRARY
DES PLAINES, ILLINOIS

02 01 00 99 98
10 9 8 7 6 5 4 3 2 1

Produced by Times Offset (M) Sdn. Bhd.

Library of Congress Cataloging-in-Publication Data

Cromwell, Sharon, 1947-
      Why does my tummy rumble when I'm hungry? : and other questions about the digestive system / by Sharon Cromwell ; photographs by Richard Smolinski, Jr.
      p.   cm.   -- (Body wise)
      Includes bibliographical references and index.
      Summary: Describes how the human digestive system works and discusses such related topics as vomiting, gas, and stomach aches.
      ISBN 1-57572-163-5 (lib.bdg.)
      1. Digestive organs--Juvenile literature.   [1. Digestive system.]
I. Smolinski, Dick , ill. II. Title. III. Series
QP145.C84   1998
612.3--dc21   97-25170
                                                                                    CIP
                                                                                    AC

Some words are shown in bold, **like this.** You can find out what they mean by looking in the glossary.

Contents

What happens to the food I eat?   4

How do I digest food?   6

Why does my tummy rumble when I'm hungry?   8

Why does my mouth water?   10

What is a burp?   12

Why do I get a tummy ache when I eat too much?   14

Why do I throw up?   16

Why do I pass gas?   18

Why do I go to the bathroom?   20

EXPLORE MORE! Your Digestive System   22

Glossary   24

More Books to Read   24

Index   24

What happens to the food I eat?

Do you know what happens to food after you chew it up and swallow it? First, it travels down your throat. Then it goes through a pipe called the **esophagus** (ih-sah-fah-gus), and into your stomach. From there, it moves through a long, tube-like **organ** called the small intestine. As it moves, the food is broken down more and more.

The food's **nutrients** are taken in through your intestine walls. Your body uses those nutrients to do things and grow. This is called **digestion**.

HEALTH FACT
The best way to get all the nutrients your body needs is to eat plenty of vegetables and fruits.

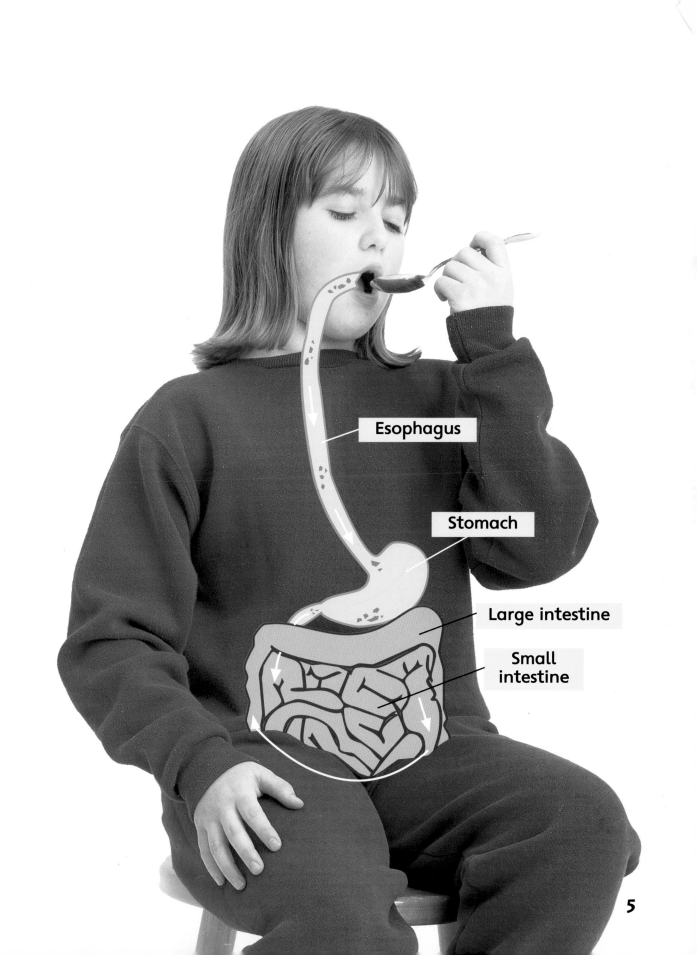

Esophagus

Stomach

Large intestine

Small
intestine

5

How do I digest food?

Digestion really begins when you start chewing. As you chew, the liquid in your mouth, called **saliva,** begins to break down food. In your stomach, other liquids break down the food even more. From your stomach, food passes into your small intestine.

Inside the small intestine, food is broken down into smaller bits. These bits are so tiny they can pass from the small intestine right into your blood vessels.

Some food cannot be digested. It passes into the large intestine. Your body then gets rid of this leftover food, or waste, through the **anus.**

HEALTH FACT

After you eat a meal, try to choose a quiet activity to do. This will help you to digest your food.

Why does my tummy rumble when I'm hungry?

Air moving around in your stomach causes rumbling that you can hear. ("Tummy" and "stomach" mean the same thing.)

HEALTH FACT

Food usually stays in your stomach for 3 to 4 hours. That's why you need to eat a meal or snack about every 4 hours during the day.

1. Your stomach and your intestines move all the time.

2. When all the food is gone from your stomach or intestines, air fills those parts of your body.

3. As muscles in your stomach and intestines move the air around, the moving air makes a rumbling sound.

4. Then your tummy rumbles, and you know you're hungry!

Stomach

Moving air

Intestines

Why does my mouth water?

The smell and taste of food often makes your mouth water with **saliva**.

1. The smell of food reaches your brain.

2. Your brain sends a message to your salivary **glands** telling them to produce saliva.

3. Once you begin to eat, chewing causes more saliva to be produced.

Brain

Salivary glands

4. Chewing and salivating, or producing saliva, are the first steps in **digestion**.

5. Chewing breaks down food into small pieces. Saliva has **enzymes** that break down starch, a substance in food.

What is a burp?

Air traveling up through your **esophagus** comes out of your mouth in a burp.

HEALTH FACT

Burps help you digest food and feel more comfortable.

1. If you swallow a lot of air when you eat, the air travels back up from your stomach because you cannot digest the air.

2. The air travels up through your esophagus and comes out of your mouth in a burp.

Esophagus

Stomach

3. You can avoid burping by chewing slowly and keeping your mouth closed while you chew.

Why do I get a tummy ache when I eat too much?

The squeezing of muscles in your stomach gives you a tummy ache.

HEALTH FACT

Fatty foods like French fries and ice cream are hard for your body to digest. If you eat meals that don't have too many fatty foods, you will feel better.

1. When you eat too much, your stomach gets very full.

2. A muscle in your stomach and muscles around your stomach **contract,** or squeeze together.

3. The squeezing of the muscles pushes some partly digested food back up out of your stomach.

4. The squeezing gives you a tummy ache.

Stomach

Why do I throw up?

A large muscle near your stomach works with the muscles in your **abdomen** to squeeze partly digested food up out of your stomach. The food travels up your **esophagus**, and out your mouth.

HEALTH FACT

Throwing up can help your body get rid of something harmful, such as spoiled food.

1. Maybe you've eaten or drunk too much too fast. A lot of partly digested food or liquid in your stomach can make you throw up.

2. When you have too much partly digested food in your stomach, it sends a message to a special part of your brain.

3. Your brain sends a message to your stomach that there is too much partly digested food in your stomach.

Brain

Esophagus

Stomach

Abdomen

4. The message goes to a very large muscle near your stomach and the muscles in the walls of your abdomen. All of these muscles squeeze together strongly. Then you throw up.

Why do I pass gas?

Bacteria in your large intestine help break down food. The bacteria and partly broken down food can sometimes produce **gas**.

HEALTH FACT

Many foods that may produce a lot of gas are very healthy. Examples are apples, broccoli, and onions.

1. You have millions of bacteria in your body. Bacteria are tiny living things that you can't see. Some bacteria are harmful. Others are helpful.

2. Helpful bacteria in your large intestine help break down food.

3. As the bacteria break down food, gas is sometimes produced.

4. When some foods, like beans, are broken down in the large intestine, a large amount of gas is produced.

5. When a lot of gas builds up, it comes out through the **anus**, the opening at the end of the large intestine.

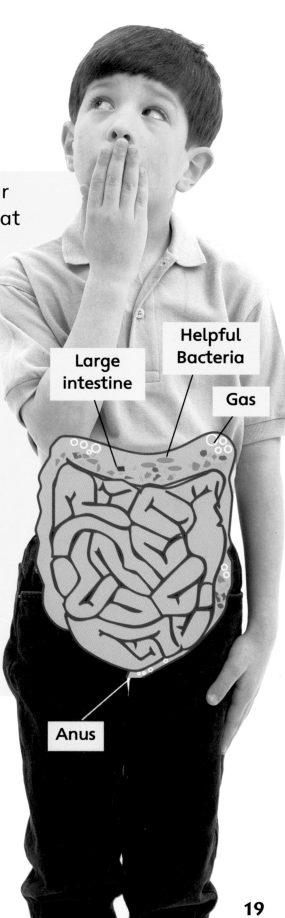

Large intestine

Helpful Bacteria

Gas

Anus

Why do I go to the bathroom?

You go to the bathroom so liquid and solid waste can leave your body.

HEALTH FACT

After you eat, it takes an average of 24 hours for **nutrients** to be absorbed by the small intestine.

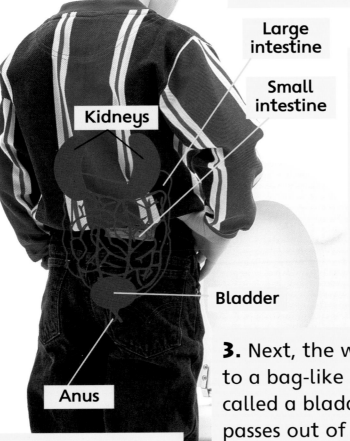

1. Liquids and solids that cannot be digested go from your small intestine to your large intestine.

Large intestine

Small intestine

Kidneys

Bladder

Anus

2. The liquid passes into your blood vessels through the walls of the large intestine. Then the liquid is taken out of your blood by a pair of **organs** called your kidneys.

3. Next, the water goes to a bag-like organ called a bladder. Then it passes out of your body as **urine**.

4. Undigested solid food is called **feces**. It comes out of your large intestine through your **anus**.

EXPLORE MORE!
Your Digestive System

1. MOUTH-WATERING MADNESS!

WHAT YOU'LL NEED:
- A handkerchief or something to use as a blindfold
- Two of your favorite foods
- One food you don't like
- A friend to help you

THEN TRY THIS!

Have your friend blindfold you. Then, one at a time, your friend should hold up a food for you to smell. Take a deep sniff. See if you salivate after smelling each food. Can you tell which foods made your mouth water the most? Did some foods not make your mouth water at all?

3. BUBBLY BURPS AND BELCHES!
WHAT YOU'LL NEED:
- Juice or water
- A bubbly drink, like seltzer or soda

THEN TRY THIS!
Take a few gulps of juice or water. Do you feel a burp inside? Then take a few gulps of something bubbly. Feel the air inside create a burp. You can let it out in a great big BURP!

2. ARE YOU A TRUE BLUE CHEWER?
WHAT YOU'LL NEED:
- Some bread to chew.

THEN TRY THIS!
Take a big bite of bread and chew it up without swallowing. Keep chewing and chewing. Soon the bread will start to taste sweet. This is because an **enzyme** in your **saliva** turns the starch in bread into sugar.

Glossary

abdomen The part of your body between the bottom of your chest and your hips.

anus The opening at the end of the large intestine.

bacteria Tiny living things that are all around you and also inside your body.

contract To make smaller by squeezing together.

digestion The breaking down of food into tiny parts.

enzymes Substances in your body that help break down food.

esophagus The tube that carries food from the throat to the stomach.

feces Undigested solid food that passes out of your body through your **anus**.

glands **Organs** that make materials for the body to use.

nutrients The things in food that keep you healthy and help you grow.

organ A part of the body that does one job.

saliva Liquid released by the **glands** in your mouth that begins the breakdown of food.

urine Liquid waste taken out of your body by the kidneys.

More Books to Read

Bailey, Donna. *All about Digestion.* Chatham, New Jersey: Raintree Steck-Vaughn, 1990.

Ganeri, Anita. *Eating.* Chatham, New Jersey: Raintree Steck-Vaughn, 1994.

Needham, Kate. *Why Do People Eat?* Tulsa, OK: Osborne, 1993.

Parker, Steve. *Eating a Meal: How You Eat, Drink, and Digest.* Danbury, CT: Franklin Watts, 1991.

Index

anus, 6, 19
bacteria, 10, 18–19
bladder, 21
blood vessels, passing of food bits into, 6
burping, 12–13, 23
esophagus, 4–5, 12–13, 16–17
feces, 21
gas, 18–19
kidneys, 21
large intestine, 5, 6, 18–19, 21
mouth, breaking down of food in, 6, 11, 23
nutrients, absorption of, 4, 6, 20
saliva, 6, 10–11, 22
small intestine, 4, 5, 6,
stomach, 4–5, 6, 13, 16–17
    aches, 14–15
    noises from, 8–9
teeth, 10
urine, 21
vomiting, 16–17
waste, removal of solid and liquid, 20–21